WILD WATERS: A FIELD GUIDE TO THE COMMON SEA MAMMALS FROM SOUTHEASTERN ALASKA

By Frederick Grant

Dedicated to Cheryl F. For giving me my first opportunity to work, learn, and grow in South Eastern Alaska.

Contents

Acknowledgments

First and foremost, I would like to thank Cheryl F from HAL for providing me with the natural history books I required to work my last season in Southeast Alaska on board the Eurodam and the Nieuw Amsterdam.

Would also like to thank the Entertainment Director Sasha from HAL for his invaluable help in setting up my lectures, and the wildlife observation times & venue on the open deck with our passengers.

Likewise, the owner of Hearthside Bookstore in Juneau, AK was so very helpful in helping me obtain the latest field guides needed to show our passengers the seabirds 'from ship to shore' of Alaska.

Plus, I would like to thank many of our past guests who had not only excellent eyesight but were also uncanny at helping me identify seabirds whilst flying. No small feat!

Lastly, I would like to thank the officers, staff, and crew from both the Eurodam and the Nieuw Amsterdam who assisted me in achieving my goals as on-board Naturalist and Alaska Wildlife Expert.

Chapter 1: Introduction to South Eastern Alaska's Sea Mammals

The Rich Biodiversity of South Eastern Alaska

South Eastern Alaska is a region renowned for its rich biodiversity and stunning natural landscapes. Nestled along the Pacific coast, this area is home to a plethora of common sea mammals, making it a haven for marine wildlife enthusiasts and nature lovers alike. In this subchapter, we will delve into the diverse array of sea mammals found in this remarkable region, highlighting their unique characteristics and the importance of their conservation.

One of the most iconic sea mammals in South Eastern Alaska is the humpback whale. Known for their majestic breaches and haunting songs, these gentle giants migrate to the region during the summer months to feed on the nutrient-rich waters. Their distinctive flippers and long, white flukes make them easily recognizable, and witnessing their acrobatic displays is a true spectacle of nature.

Another common sea mammal found in these waters is the Steller sea lion. These charismatic creatures, with their thick fur and large, dark bodies, are a favorite among visitors to the region. Steller sea lions are known for their playful behavior and can often be spotted basking on rocky shores or gracefully swimming through the waves. However, due to habitat loss and overfishing, they are now considered a threatened species, emphasizing the need for conservation efforts.

South Eastern Alaska is also home to several species of seals, including the harbor seal and the spotted seal. Harbor seals, with their wide-eyed expressions and sleek bodies, can often be seen lounging on ice floes or rocky outcrops. Spotted seals, on the other hand, are characterized by their distinctive black spots and unique vocalizations. These seals play an essential role in maintaining the delicate balance of the marine ecosystem and are a vital part of the region's biodiversity.

In addition to these well-known sea mammals, South Eastern Alaska is teeming with other fascinating creatures such as orcas, Dall's porpoises, and sea otters. Each species contributes to the intricate web of life in this region, and their presence is a testament to the importance of preserving the natural environment.

As responsible stewards of this planet, it is our duty to protect and conserve the rich biodiversity found in South Eastern Alaska. Understanding the unique characteristics and behaviors of these common sea mammals is the first step towards fostering a deep appreciation for their existence. By raising awareness and supporting conservation initiatives, we can ensure that generations to come will have the opportunity to marvel at the splendor of these remarkable creatures and the incredible natural wonders of South Eastern Alaska.

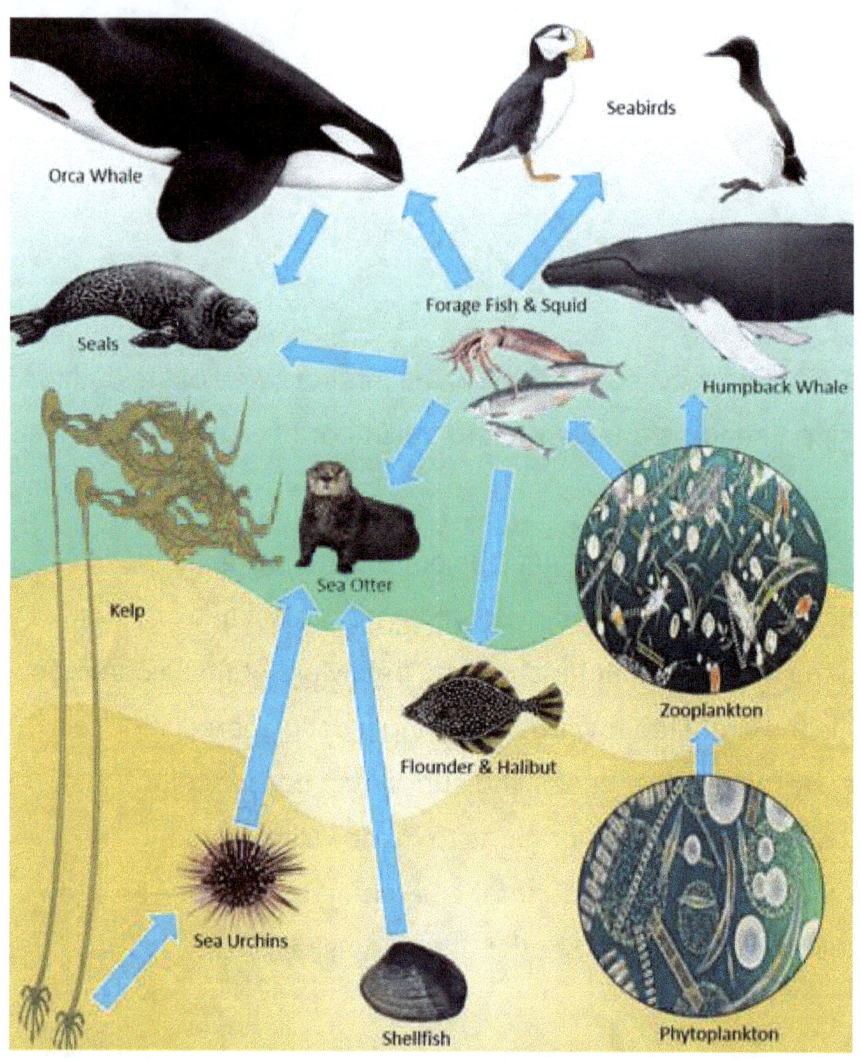

Importance of Sea Mammals in the Ecosystem

Sea mammals play a crucial role in maintaining the delicate balance of the marine ecosystem in South Eastern Alaska. These magnificent creatures, including whales, seals, sea lions, and otters, contribute to the overall health and diversity of the region's waters. In this subchapter, we will explore the significance of sea mammals and their impact on the ecosystem.

One of the primary roles of sea mammals is their influence on the food chain. They occupy various trophic levels, serving as both predators and prey. For instance, whales, such as the humpback and killer whales, feed on fish and krill, helping to control their populations. This, in turn, prevents an overabundance of certain species, ensuring the ecosystem remains in equilibrium. Additionally, sea mammals like seals and sea lions provide prey for larger predators, such as sharks and orcas, further balancing the marine food web.

Furthermore, the presence of sea mammals contributes to nutrient cycling. These creatures often migrate vast distances, traveling from nutrient-rich feeding grounds to breeding areas. As they travel, they excrete waste, which contains essential nutrients. This waste acts as a natural fertilizer, promoting the growth of phytoplankton and other microscopic organisms. These tiny organisms form the base of the marine food chain, ultimately supporting a diverse array of marine life, including fish, crustaceans, and other sea mammals.

Sea mammals also have a significant impact on coastal ecosystems. Sea otters, for example, play a crucial role in maintaining kelp forests. They feed on sea urchins, which are known to devour kelp. By keeping the sea urchin population in check, otters preserve the kelp forests, which provide crucial habitats for a multitude of marine species. These underwater forests also act as carbon sinks, absorbing carbon dioxide from the atmosphere and helping to mitigate the impacts of climate change.

Beyond their ecological importance, sea mammals also hold cultural and economic value for the people of South Eastern Alaska. They have been an integral part of indigenous cultures for centuries, providing sustenance and spiritual significance. Additionally, whale watching and wildlife tourism have become major sources of income for local communities, attracting visitors from around the world who seek to witness the beauty and grandeur of these creatures in their natural habitat.

In conclusion, sea mammals are vital components of the South Eastern Alaskan ecosystem. Their role in regulating the food chain, promoting nutrient cycling, and maintaining coastal habitats is crucial for the overall health and diversity of the marine environment. Understanding and appreciating the importance of these common sea mammals is essential for the conservation and sustainable management of this unique and awe-inspiring ecosystem.

Overview of Sea Mammal Research in the Region

Sea mammals are an integral part of the diverse ecosystem found in South Eastern Alaska. From majestic whales to playful seals and sea lions, these remarkable creatures capture our imagination and inspire a sense of wonder. Understanding their behaviors, habitats, and conservation needs is crucial for ensuring the long-term viability of these species and the delicate balance of the marine environment they inhabit.

This subchapter aims to provide an overview of the extensive research conducted on sea mammals in South Eastern Alaska. By delving into the fascinating world of these common sea mammals, we hope to foster a deeper appreciation for their role in the region's ecosystem and the challenges they face.

Scientists and researchers have dedicated countless hours to studying the behavior, migration patterns, reproductive cycles, and feeding habits of sea mammals in this area. By employing advanced techniques such as satellite tagging, acoustic monitoring, and genetic analysis, they have been able to gather invaluable data on these magnificent creatures.

One of the primary goals of this research is to understand the impact of human activities on sea mammal populations. By collecting data on noise pollution, habitat destruction, and changes in food availability, scientists can better assess the threats these animals face and develop effective conservation strategies.

Another area of research focuses on the interplay between sea mammals and their environment. By studying the complex relationships between predators and prey, scientists can gain insights into the health of the ecosystem as a whole. This research also helps identify critical areas that require protection, such as important feeding and breeding grounds.

Furthermore, ongoing research efforts aim to unravel the mysteries of sea mammal communication and social structures. By decoding their vocalizations and observing their social behavior, scientists can gain a deeper understanding of how these animals interact and communicate with one another.

This subchapter will explore the findings of these research endeavors, highlighting key discoveries and shedding light on the ongoing efforts to conserve and protect sea mammals in South Eastern Alaska. By understanding the challenges faced by these remarkable creatures, we can all play a part in ensuring their survival and the preservation of the unique marine ecosystem they call home.

Whether you are a nature enthusiast, a student, or simply curious about the sea mammals of South Eastern Alaska, this subchapter will provide you with a comprehensive overview of the research conducted in the region. Join us on this journey of discovery and gain a deeper appreciation for the common sea mammals that grace the wild waters of South Eastern Alaska.

Chapter 2: Understanding Sea Mammal Anatomy and Physiology

Adaptations for Life in the Ocean

The ocean is a vast and challenging environment, but the sea mammals of Southeastern Alaska have evolved remarkable adaptations that allow them to thrive in these wild waters. In this subchapter, we will explore the unique characteristics and behaviors of these fascinating creatures.

One of the most remarkable adaptations of sea mammals is their ability to regulate body temperature. Unlike humans, who are homeothermic and maintain a constant body temperature, sea mammals are poikilothermic, meaning their body temperature varies with the temperature of their surroundings. This adaptation allows them to conserve energy in the cold waters of Alaska, where temperatures can plummet. Species like the Steller sea lion and Harbor seal have thick layers of blubber that act as insulation, keeping them warm even in freezing temperatures.

Another adaptation essential for life in the ocean is the ability to hold their breath for extended periods. Sea mammals have specialized lungs that allow them to take in and store large amounts of oxygen. This enables them to remain submerged for extended periods while hunting for food or escaping predators. The Humpback whale, for example, can hold its breath for up to 60 minutes, allowing it to dive deep into the ocean in search of krill and small fish.

Sea mammals have also developed unique feeding strategies tailored to their marine environment. The Orca, or killer whale, is a prime example of a specialized predator. It uses sophisticated hunting techniques, such as cooperative hunting in pods, to catch prey. These intelligent creatures have even been observed intentionally beaching themselves to snatch seals off the shoreline.

Additionally, sea mammals have adapted their senses to excel in underwater environments. Many species, like the Dall's porpoise, have excellent eyesight, allowing them to navigate and spot prey even in dimly lit waters. Some, such as the Beluga whale, have developed echolocation, emitting high-frequency sounds and using the echoes to locate objects and navigate through the ocean depths.

In conclusion, the sea mammals of Southeastern Alaska have evolved a remarkable array of adaptations to survive and thrive in their oceanic home. From specialized temperature regulation to unique feeding strategies and sensory adaptations, these creatures have truly mastered the art of ocean living. By understanding and appreciating these adaptations, we can develop a deeper respect for these magnificent creatures and the delicate ecosystems they call home.

Distinguishing Features of Sea Mammals

When exploring the vast and breathtaking waters of South Eastern Alaska, one is bound to encounter a diverse array of sea mammals. These magnificent creatures have adapted to life in the ocean, boasting a range of distinguishing features that set them apart from their terrestrial counterparts. In this subchapter, we will delve into the unique characteristics of the common sea mammals found in this region, providing a comprehensive understanding of their fascinating adaptations.

One of the most recognizable sea mammals in South Eastern Alaska is the humpback whale. These gentle giants can reach lengths of up to 50 feet and are known for their distinctive long pectoral fins and knobby protrusions on their heads called tubercles. These tubercles house hair follicles, which are believed to enhance the whale's sense of touch. Humpback whales are also famous for their acrobatic displays, leaping out of the water and slapping their tails against the surface, a behavior known as "breaching."

Another common sea mammal in these Alaskan waters is the harbor seal. These sleek animals have a streamlined body shape, enabling them to navigate through the water with ease. Their short, powerful flippers and agile movements make them adept hunters, preying on fish and crustaceans that inhabit the region. One distinguishing feature of the harbor seal is its large, expressive eyes, which allow for excellent underwater vision.

Moving on to the orca, or killer whale, we find a highly intelligent and social species. Orcas have a striking black and white coloration, with a tall dorsal fin on their backs. These apex predators have sharp teeth that they use to capture a variety of prey, including fish, seals, and even other whales. Orcas are known for their complex vocalizations, using distinct calls and whistles to communicate within their pods.

Lastly, the sea otter is a beloved sea mammal found in South Eastern Alaska. These playful creatures have thick, dense fur that helps insulate them in the chilly waters. Sea otters are skilled at using rocks as tools to crack open shells and feed on mollusks. They can often be observed floating on their backs, using their bellies as a table for their meals.

Understanding the distinguishing features of these common sea mammals of South Eastern Alaska allows us to appreciate their incredible adaptations to life in the ocean. Whether it's the humpback whale's tubercles, the harbor seal's expressive eyes, the orca's black and white coloration, or the sea otter's tool-using behavior, each species has its own unique characteristics that make them truly remarkable. So, keep your eyes peeled as you venture into these wild waters, and you may just catch a glimpse of these extraordinary creatures in their natural habitat.

Reproduction and Life Cycle

In the vast and diverse ecosystem of South Eastern Alaska, common sea mammals play a vital role. These fascinating creatures have adapted to the harsh marine environment and have developed unique reproductive strategies to ensure the survival of their species. This subchapter will delve into the intricacies of their reproduction and life cycle.

One of the most awe-inspiring sights in South Eastern Alaska is witnessing the birth of a sea mammal. From the majestic humpback whales to the adorable harbor seals, these mammals undergo a fascinating reproductive process. Most sea mammals are viviparous, meaning they give birth to live young ones. The gestation period varies among species, with some lasting for several months, while others can extend up to a year.

For many common sea mammals of South Eastern Alaska, such as Killer Whales and sea lions, reproduction occurs in specific breeding seasons. During this time, males compete fiercely for the attention of females through displays of dominance and vocalizations. Once a female accepts a mate, she will give birth to a single offspring, known as a pup or calf, after the gestation period.

The early stages of life for sea mammals are crucial for their survival. Pups are born fully formed and are dependent on their mothers for nourishment and protection. They develop quickly, learning to swim and hunt within a few months. This period of dependency can last from a few weeks to several years, depending on the species.

As the young sea mammals grow, they go through various stages of development, acquiring the skills needed for survival in the challenging marine environment. They learn to navigate the treacherous waters, hunt for food, and communicate with their fellow pod members.

Reproduction and life cycles of common sea mammals in South Eastern Alaska are tightly intertwined with the dynamic ecosystem they inhabit. These creatures have evolved over centuries, adapting to the ever-changing conditions of their environment. By understanding their reproductive strategies and life cycles, we can appreciate the remarkable resilience and beauty of these magnificent creatures.

Whether you are a nature enthusiast, a researcher, or simply someone curious about the common sea mammals of South Eastern Alaska, this subchapter will provide you with valuable insights into their reproduction and life cycles. Prepare to be amazed by the wonders of nature as we explore the intricacies of these extraordinary creatures in Wild Waters: A Field Guide to the Common Sea Mammals of South Eastern Alaska.

Chapter 3: Cetaceans: Whales, Dolphins, and Porpoises

Humpback Whales (Megaptera novaeangliae)

Humpback whales, scientifically known as Megaptera novaeangliae, are one of the most majestic creatures that grace the waters of South Eastern Alaska. These magnificent giants are a common sight in the region and have captured the hearts and imaginations of both locals and visitors alike. In this subchapter, we will delve into the fascinating world of humpback whales, exploring their physical characteristics, behavior, and the crucial role they play in the marine ecosystem.

Physical Characteristics:

Humpback whales are known for their impressive size, reaching lengths of up to 50 feet and weighing around 40 tons. Their bodies are streamlined, with long pectoral fins that can span up to 15 feet. These fins are unique to each individual whale, acting as a fingerprint and enabling researchers to identify and track them. One of the most striking features of humpback whales is their long, slender flukes, which they often raise high above the water when diving.

Behavior:

Humpback whales are renowned for their acrobatic displays, often breaching, lobtailing, or slapping their tails on the water's surface. These behaviors serve various purposes, including communication, courtship rituals, and possibly even removing parasites. These breathtaking displays are a sight to behold and are a common occurrence in the waters of South Eastern Alaska.

Ecosystem Role:

Humpback whales play a vital role in maintaining the delicate balance of the marine ecosystem. These gentle giants are filter feeders, primarily consuming krill and small fish. Their feeding habits help control the population of these prey species, preventing them from overwhelming the ecosystem. Additionally, humpback whales are known to engage in a behavior called bubble net feeding, where a group of whales forms a circle and releases bubbles to corral their prey. This cooperative feeding technique is a testament to their intelligence and social nature.

Conservation Efforts:

Despite being a common sight in South Eastern Alaska, humpback whales face several threats, including entanglement in fishing gear, ship strikes, and habitat degradation. To ensure the long-term survival of these magnificent creatures, various conservation efforts have been put into place, including protected areas, strict regulations on fishing practices, and public awareness campaigns.

In conclusion, humpback whales are an integral part of the South Eastern Alaska marine ecosystem, captivating all who have the privilege of witnessing their awe-inspiring presence. By understanding their physical characteristics, behavior, and conservation status, we can all play a part in ensuring the preservation of these incredible creatures for generations to come.

Orca Whales (Orcinus orca)

The majestic Orca Whales, also known as killer whales, are a prominent and fascinating species found in the wild waters of South Eastern Alaska. In this subchapter, we will explore the incredible world of these common sea mammals, providing insight into their behavior, habitat, and significance to the ecosystem.

Orca whales are highly intelligent and social creatures that captivate the imagination of everyone who encounters them. With their distinctive black and white markings and impressive size, they are easily recognizable. These magnificent creatures are the largest members of the dolphin family and are known for their powerful and graceful swimming abilities.

Found in the cool, nutrient-rich waters of South Eastern Alaska, Orca whales play a vital role in maintaining the balance of the marine ecosystem. They are apex predators and occupy the top of the food chain, feeding on a variety of marine animals, including fish, seals, and even other whales. Their hunting techniques involve remarkable teamwork and strategic planning, making them one of nature's most efficient predators.

The social structure of Orca whales is another intriguing aspect of their behavior. They live in matrilineal pods, consisting of several generations of related individuals led by a matriarch. These pods communicate through a complex system of clicks, whistles, and vocalizations, which helps them coordinate hunting, navigate, and maintain social bonds. Their strong family ties and cooperative nature add to the awe-inspiring nature of these magnificent creatures.

South Eastern Alaska's waters provide a rich and diverse habitat for Orca whales, offering ample food sources and shelter. They are known to undertake long migrations, following the seasonal movement of their prey. These migrations often bring them close to the shores of South Eastern Alaska, providing an excellent opportunity for locals and visitors to witness their astounding displays of breaching, spy-hopping, and tail-slapping.

Preserving the habitat and ensuring the well-being of Orca whales is of utmost importance. The book, "Wild Waters: A Field Guide to the Common Sea Mammals of South Eastern Alaska," aims to educate and raise awareness about the importance of conserving these incredible creatures and their environment. By understanding their behavior, habitat, and significance in the ecosystem, we can work together to protect and appreciate the Orca whales for generations to come.

Whether you are a nature enthusiast, a local resident, or a visitor to the beautiful region of South Eastern Alaska, learning about Orca whales will undoubtedly deepen your appreciation for these magnificent creatures and the delicate balance of the marine ecosystem they call home.

Dall's Porpoises (Phocoenoides dalli)

Dall's Porpoises are some of the most fascinating and charismatic sea mammals found in the waters of South Eastern Alaska. With their sleek bodies and playful nature, these porpoises never fail to capture the hearts of both locals and visitors alike. In this subchapter, we will delve deeper into the world of Dall's Porpoises, exploring their physical characteristics, behavior, and the importance of their conservation.

Physical Characteristics:

Dall's Porpoises are small cetaceans, measuring approximately six to eight feet in length and weighing around 300 pounds. They have a distinctive black and white coloration, with a dark dorsal side and a white belly. This unique color pattern often leads to them being mistaken for killer whales or baby belugas from a distance. Their bodies are robust and torpedo-shaped, allowing them to swim at impressive speeds.

Behavior:

These porpoises are known for their incredible agility and playful behavior. They are often observed riding the bow waves created by boats, performing acrobatic leaps and somersaults. Dall's Porpoises are also highly social creatures, traveling in small groups of two to 12 individuals, known as pods. These pods are typically composed of family members, and they communicate with each other using a series of clicks and whistles.

Conservation:

While Dall's Porpoises are not currently considered endangered, they face several threats that require our attention. One of the biggest concerns is accidental entanglement in fishing gear, particularly gillnets. These porpoises are known to be curious and may investigate floating objects, putting them at risk of becoming entangled. Additionally, pollution, habitat degradation, and noise pollution from maritime activities can have a significant impact on their well-being.

To ensure the long-term survival of Dall's Porpoises, it is crucial that we take steps to protect their habitat and reduce human-induced threats. This includes advocating for responsible fishing practices, such as the use of alternative fishing gear that minimizes the risk of accidental entanglement. Implementing stricter regulations to control pollution and noise pollution in their habitats is also essential.

By spreading awareness about the importance of Dall's Porpoises and engaging in conservation efforts, we can help preserve the rich biodiversity of South Eastern Alaska's waters. Whether you are a local resident, a visitor, or simply someone interested in sea mammals, it is our collective responsibility to ensure the survival of these magnificent creatures for generations to come.

Harbor Porpoises (Phocoena phocoena)

Harbor porpoises, scientifically known as Phocoena phocoena, are one of the most common sea mammals found in the waters of South Eastern Alaska. These fascinating creatures, often referred to as "the puffins of the sea," captivate both scientists and nature enthusiasts alike. In this subchapter, we will explore the unique characteristics and behaviors of harbor porpoises, shedding light on their importance in the intricate ecosystem of South Eastern Alaska.

Harbor porpoises are small cetaceans, measuring about 5 to 6 feet in length and weighing around 150 pounds. Their bodies are streamlined, allowing them to effortlessly glide through the water at speeds of up to 25 miles per hour. With a dark gray dorsal side and a lighter gray or white underside, they possess a distinct coloration that aids in their camouflage from predators.

These porpoises are highly social animals, forming small groups known as pods. Within these pods, they communicate using a series of clicks and whistles, allowing them to navigate and locate prey efficiently. Unlike other cetaceans, harbor porpoises have a shy nature, often avoiding boats and humans. However, lucky observers may catch a glimpse of their playful behavior, including leaping and riding the bow waves of passing vessels.

Feeding primarily on small fish and squid, harbor porpoises play a vital role in maintaining the balance of the marine ecosystem. Their consumption of abundant prey helps control the population of these smaller species, preventing overgrowth and potential disruptions in the food chain. As such, their presence is crucial in preserving the biodiversity of South Eastern Alaska's waters.

Despite their important ecological role, harbor porpoises face several challenges. Habitat degradation, pollution, and entanglement in fishing gear pose significant threats to their population. Conservation efforts, such as establishing protected areas and implementing sustainable fishing practices, are crucial to ensure the survival of these remarkable creatures.

In conclusion, harbor porpoises hold a special place in South Eastern Alaska's marine ecosystem. Their small size belies their importance, as they contribute to the delicate balance of the underwater world. By raising awareness about these remarkable sea mammals and promoting their conservation, we can safeguard their future and preserve the natural wonders of South Eastern Alaska for generations to come.

Pacific White-Sided Dolphins (Lagenorhynchus obliquidens)

Pacific White-Sided Dolphins are a common sight in the waters of Southeastern Alaska, captivating both locals and tourists alike. With their striking black, white, and gray coloration and playful behavior, these beautiful creatures have become one of the most beloved sea mammals in the region.

Physical Characteristics:

Pacific White-Sided Dolphins are medium-sized dolphins, measuring between 5 and 8 feet in length and weighing around 300 to 400 pounds. They have a robust body with a short, pointed snout and a well-defined beak. Their most distinctive feature is their tri-colored pattern, with a dark gray or black back, a white belly, and a light gray or white patch on their sides. This unique coloring sets them apart from other dolphin species in the area.

Behavior and Habitat:

These dolphins are highly social and often travel in groups of up to 100 individuals, known as pods. They are known for their acrobatic displays, leaping out of the water, riding the bow waves created by boats, and even somersaulting in the air. These playful behaviors make them a favorite among wildlife enthusiasts.

Pacific White-Sided Dolphins are primarily found in the cool temperate waters of the North Pacific Ocean. They are commonly seen in the coastal waters of Southeastern Alaska, where they feed on a variety of fish and squid species. These dolphins are known to travel long distances in search of food, often following schools of fish or other cetaceans.

Conservation:

While Pacific White-Sided Dolphins are not currently considered endangered, they face threats from human activities such as pollution, habitat degradation, and entanglement in fishing gear. It is crucial for us to protect their habitat and ensure sustainable fishing practices to preserve these magnificent creatures for future generations to enjoy.

Encountering Pacific White-Sided Dolphins in the wild is an awe-inspiring experience. Their energetic nature and stunning coloration make them true icons of Southeastern Alaska's marine ecosystem. So, whether you're a resident or a visitor to this beautiful region, keep an eye out for these playful dolphins, and cherish the opportunity to witness their grace and beauty in their natural habitat.

Harbor Seals (Phoca vitulina)

Harbor seals, scientifically known as Phoca vitulina, are one of the most common sea mammals found in the pristine waters of Southeastern Alaska. These adorable creatures captivate both locals and tourists alike with their playful antics and distinctive appearance. In this subchapter, we will explore the fascinating world of harbor seals, shedding light on their characteristics, behavior, and the importance of their presence in the region.

Harbor seals are medium-sized pinnipeds that inhabit coastal areas, including estuaries, bays, and fjords. Their sleek bodies are well-adapted for life in the water, with streamlined shapes and thick blubber that helps them regulate body temperature in the cold Alaskan waters. They have short, powerful flippers that enable them to navigate effortlessly through the currents, making them excellent swimmers.

One of the most distinctive features of harbor seals is their adorable appearance. They have round heads with large, expressive eyes, giving them a perpetually curious and innocent look. Their coats come in a variety of colors, ranging from light gray to dark brown, and they often have unique patterns of spots and rings. These markings are not only aesthetically pleasing but also help individual seals identify each other.

Harbor seals are known for their playful nature. They can often be seen basking on rocky outcrops or floating on chunks of ice, engaging in various social behaviors. Play-fighting, vocalizing, and even somersaulting are common activities among these social creatures. They also communicate through a range of vocalizations, including barks, growls, and trills, which are essential for maintaining social bonds and territorial defense.

As an integral part of the marine ecosystem in Southeastern Alaska, harbor seals play a vital role in maintaining the balance of the region's biodiversity. They are opportunistic feeders, primarily consuming fish, squid, and crustaceans. By regulating their prey populations, harbor seals help maintain healthy fish stocks and contribute to the overall health of the coastal ecosystem.

Understanding and appreciating the presence of harbor seals in South Eastern Alaska is crucial for everyone, whether you are a local resident, a nature enthusiast, or a curious visitor. Observing these charming creatures in their natural habitat provides a unique opportunity to connect with the wonders of the marine world. So, next time you find yourself near the beautiful waters of Southeastern Alaska, keep an eye out for these lovable harbor seals, and prepare to be enchanted by their presence.

Steller Sea Lions (Eumetopias jubatus)

Steller Sea Lions, also known as Northern Sea Lions, are one of the most recognizable and charismatic sea mammals found in the waters of South Eastern Alaska. These majestic creatures are the largest of all sea lions, with adult males reaching lengths of up to 11 feet and weighing as much as 2,500 pounds. Their distinctive features include a thick neck, a broad and flat head, and a luxuriant mane of coarse, dark brown hair.

One of the key distinguishing factors of Steller Sea Lions is their territorial nature. They establish breeding colonies on remote rocky shores, where they congregate in large numbers during the summer months. These colonies can consist of hundreds or even thousands of individuals, creating a bustling and noisy environment. Each male defends his territory fiercely, often engaging in loud vocalizations and physical displays to establish dominance and attract females.

Steller Sea Lions are highly adaptable hunters, capable of catching a wide variety of prey. Their diet primarily consists of fish, such as salmon, herring, and cod, but they have also been known to feast on squid and octopus. With their remarkable swimming abilities, they can dive to impressive depths of up to 1,500 feet in search of food, holding their breath for several minutes at a time.

Despite their impressive size and strength, Steller Sea Lions face numerous threats in the wild. Overfishing has led to a decline in their food sources, making it harder for them to find enough sustenance to survive. Pollution and habitat destruction also pose significant risks to their population. Conservation efforts have been initiated to protect these magnificent creatures, including the establishment of marine protected areas and regulations on fishing practices.

Observing Steller Sea Lions in their natural habitat is a truly awe-inspiring experience. Their playful nature and agility in the water make them a joy to watch. Their distinct vocalizations, ranging from deep roars to high-pitched barks, add to the enchantment of encountering them. Whether you are a wildlife enthusiast, a nature lover, or simply curious about the common sea mammals of South Eastern Alaska, the Steller Sea Lion is a captivating creature that deserves admiration and protection.

Northern Fur Seals (Callorhinus ursinus)

The northern fur seal, scientifically known as Callorhinus ursinus, is a captivating marine mammal found in the coastal waters of South Eastern Alaska. These charismatic creatures are known for their luxurious fur coats and unique behaviors, making them a popular sight among wildlife enthusiasts and researchers alike.

Physical Characteristics:

Northern fur seals are medium-sized pinnipeds, with adult males reaching lengths of up to 6.5 feet and weighing between 400 and 600 pounds. Females, on the other hand, are smaller, measuring around 4.5 feet and weighing between 80 and 120 pounds. Their bodies are well-adapted for life in the ocean, featuring a streamlined shape and strong flippers for efficient swimming.

Distinctive Features:

One of the most distinguishing features of northern fur seals is their thick, water-repellent fur, which gives them their name. Males display a dark brown to black coat, while females exhibit a lighter, grayish-brown coloration. Another notable characteristic is the males' large size compared to the females, giving them a distinctive appearance during breeding season.

Behavior and Habitat:

Northern fur seals are highly social animals, often forming large aggregations called rookeries during the breeding season. These rookeries can consist of thousands of individuals, creating a cacophony of barks and calls. Outside of the breeding season, they are known to migrate thousands of miles to find food, often diving to great depths in search of squid, fish, and other marine prey.

Conservation Status:

While once heavily hunted for their pelts, the northern fur seal population has seen a significant recovery since the implementation of protective measures. However, they still face threats such as climate change, pollution, and entanglement in fishing gear. Conservation efforts continue to monitor and protect these remarkable creatures to ensure their long-term survival.

Observing Northern Fur Seals:

If you're fortunate enough to visit the coastal waters of South Eastern Alaska, keep an eye out for these mesmerizing creatures. You may spot them lounging on rocky shores or swimming gracefully in the ocean. Remember to maintain a safe distance to avoid disturbing their natural behaviors and always adhere to wildlife viewing guidelines.

In conclusion, northern fur seals are fascinating marine mammals that call the coastal waters of South Eastern Alaska their home. Their unique physical characteristics, distinct behaviors, and ongoing conservation efforts make them a significant part of the region's diverse ecosystem. Enjoy the privilege of observing these magnificent creatures while respecting their natural habitat and contributing to their ongoing protection.

California Sea Lions (Zalophus californianus)

The California Sea Lion, scientifically known as Zalophus californianus, is a fascinating and charismatic marine mammal that can be found along the coasts of South Eastern Alaska. This subchapter provides an in-depth look at these common sea mammals, offering valuable information for everyone interested in the wildlife of this region.

Physical Characteristics:

California Sea Lions are easily identifiable by their sleek and agile bodies. Males are larger than females, reaching lengths of up to 8 feet and weighing around 800 pounds. Females are slightly smaller, measuring about 6 feet in length and weighing around 250 pounds. They have a distinctive brown or tan-colored fur, with males often developing a darker hue as they mature. Their long, slender flippers make them excellent swimmers, and their streamlined bodies allow them to move swiftly through the water.

Habitat and Range:

These sea lions are highly adaptable and can be found in a variety of habitats. They primarily inhabit rocky coastlines, sandy beaches, and offshore islands from South Eastern Alaska South to central Mexico. Main breeding colonies are located off of the Channel Islands, California to central Mexico, as these coastal waters are rich in fish and other marine life. During breeding season, large numbers of California Sea Lions congregate on beaches and rocky outcrops, creating a boisterous and energetic atmosphere.

Behavior and Diet:

California Sea Lions are known for their social nature and can often be seen in large groups, both on land and in the water. They are excellent swimmers and divers, capable of reaching depths of up to 900 feet in search of prey. Their diet mainly consists of fish, including herring, salmon, and anchovies, as well as squid and octopus. These sea lions are also known to be opportunistic feeders, often scavenging from fishing vessels or stealing catches from other marine mammals.

Conservation Status:

While California Sea Lions are not currently considered endangered, they face various threats in their natural habitat. Pollution, habitat loss, entanglement in fishing gear, and illegal hunting all pose significant challenges to their survival. It is important for everyone to be aware of these issues and actively support conservation efforts to protect these remarkable creatures for future generations.

In conclusion, the California Sea Lion is an integral part of the diverse marine ecosystem found in South Eastern Alaska. Their unique characteristics, behavior, and habitat make them a captivating subject for anyone interested in the common sea mammals of this region. By understanding and appreciating these magnificent creatures, we can contribute to their conservation and ensure their long-term survival in the wild waters of Alaska.

Chapter 5: Sea Otters: The Charismatic Keystone Species

The Importance of Sea Otters in South Eastern Alaska

Sea otters are among the most fascinating and important sea mammals found in the waters of South Eastern Alaska. These charming creatures play a crucial role in maintaining the delicate ecological balance of this region. In this subchapter, we will explore the significance of sea otters and their impact on the marine ecosystem.

One of the primary reasons sea otters are vital to South Eastern Alaska is their role as a keystone species. They have a unique and profound effect on the overall health and biodiversity of the region. By feeding on sea urchins, crabs, and other invertebrates, sea otters help control their populations, preventing them from overgrazing and damaging kelp forests.

These kelp forests serve as essential habitats for numerous fish species, providing shelter, food, and breeding grounds. Without sea otters, these ecosystems would suffer, leading to a cascade of negative effects on the entire food web.

Moreover, sea otters are known for their remarkable ability to maintain their fur's insulating properties by grooming it meticulously. This behavior helps keep them warm in the frigid waters of South Eastern Alaska. However, it also has a significant impact on the health of the local marine environment. Sea otters' grooming habits result in the release of oils into the water, which helps disperse nutrients and promote the growth of phytoplankton. Phytoplankton, in turn, serves as the foundation of the marine food chain, supporting the growth of zooplankton, fish, and other marine organisms.

Sea otters also contribute to the economy of South Eastern Alaska through ecotourism. People from all around the world visit this region to catch a glimpse of these charismatic creatures in their natural habitat. This tourism industry generates revenue for local communities, supporting jobs and businesses. The presence of sea otters in the area enhances the overall appeal of South Eastern Alaska as a destination for wildlife enthusiasts and nature lovers.

In conclusion, sea otters are of utmost importance to the marine ecosystems of South Eastern Alaska. As keystone species, they help maintain the balance and health of the region's delicate food web by controlling populations of their prey. Their grooming habits also contribute to the growth of phytoplankton, which sustains the entire marine ecosystem. Additionally, sea otters play a significant role in the local economy through ecotourism. Understanding and appreciating the vital role of sea otters is crucial for the conservation and preservation of South Eastern Alaska's diverse marine life.

Behavior and Habitat of Sea Otters

Sea otters are fascinating marine mammals found in the coastal waters of South Eastern Alaska. Known for their playful nature and unique adaptations, they have captured the hearts of both locals and tourists alike. In this subchapter, we will explore the behavior and habitat of these delightful creatures, shedding light on their role in the ecosystem and their survival strategies.

Sea otters spend most of their time in the water, rarely coming ashore. They are excellent swimmers, using their webbed feet and sleek bodies to navigate through the chilly waters with ease. Their dense fur, which consists of around one million hairs per square inch, provides incredible insulation and buoyancy, keeping them warm in the frigid Alaskan waters. It also requires constant grooming to maintain its insulating properties.

These social animals are often observed in groups called rafts, which can range in size from a few individuals to hundreds. Rafts not only provide protection against predators but also facilitate social interactions and cooperative foraging. Sea otters are known for their playful behavior, frequently seen rolling, diving, and even using tools. They use rocks to smash open hard-shelled prey, such as clams and mussels, showcasing their intelligence and resourcefulness.

Sea otters primarily inhabit nearshore coastal areas, including kelp forests, estuaries, and rocky shores. Kelp forests serve as important habitats for these mammals, providing both food and shelter. Sea otters have a strong affinity for kelp, often wrapping themselves in the seaweed to prevent drifting off while they rest or groom. They also use kelp as a tool to anchor themselves during feeding, enabling them to search for food without being carried away by the current.

The presence of sea otters has a significant impact on the ecosystem. By feeding on sea urchins and other invertebrates, they help maintain the balance of kelp forests. Without sea otters, sea urchin populations can explode, leading to the overgrazing of kelp, which in turn negatively affects the abundance and diversity of other marine species. Therefore, sea otters are considered a keystone species, playing a crucial role in shaping the coastal ecosystem of South Eastern Alaska.

In conclusion, sea otters are charismatic and important members of the marine community in South Eastern Alaska. Their playful behavior, reliance on kelp forests, and ecological significance make them a captivating subject for study and admiration. Whether you are a nature enthusiast, a scientist, or simply someone looking to learn more about the common sea mammals of South Eastern Alaska, understanding the behavior and habitat of sea otters is a must.

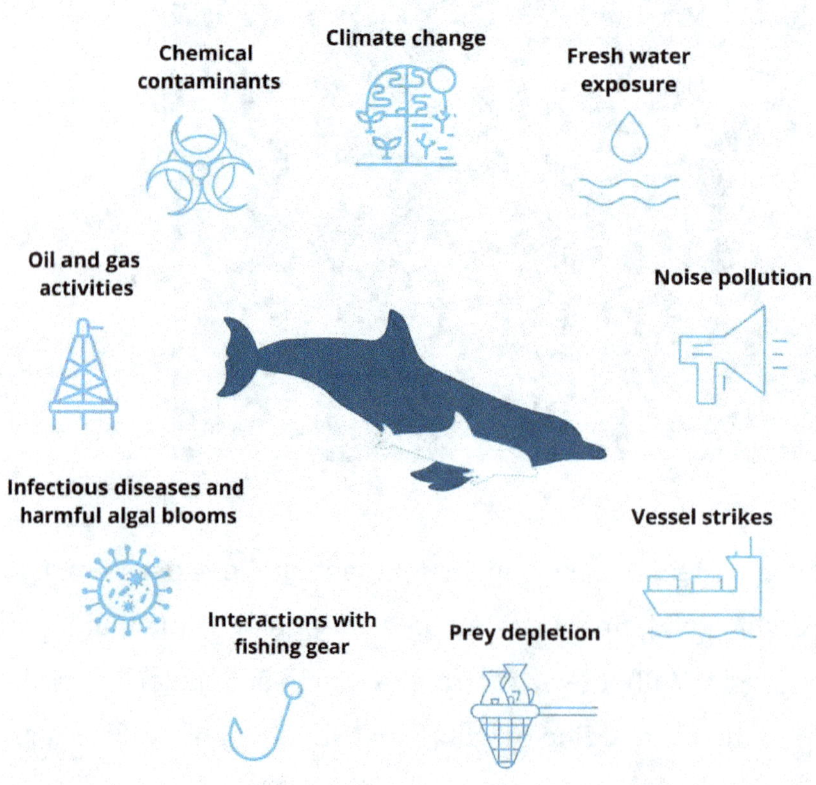

Threats and Conservation Efforts

The breathtaking waters of South Eastern Alaska are home to a diverse range of common sea mammals, captivating both locals and visitors alike. These remarkable creatures, such as seals, sea lions, and whales, play a vital role in the delicate ecosystem of this extraordinary region. However, their existence is increasingly threatened by various factors, highlighting the urgent need for conservation efforts to safeguard their populations and their habitats.

One of the primary threats faced by common sea mammals in South Eastern Alaska is the loss of their natural habitat. Rapid urbanization and industrial development have resulted in habitat destruction and fragmentation, leaving these magnificent creatures with limited space to thrive. Pollution is another grave concern, with oil spills and chemical contaminants posing significant risks to the health and survival of sea mammals. These pollutants not only contaminate their food sources but also directly impact their reproductive capabilities and overall well-being.

Overfishing is yet another critical threat to the sea mammals of this region. The depletion of fish stocks, which form a substantial part of the diet for many marine mammals, can lead to malnutrition and starvation. Additionally, entanglement in fishing gear and accidental capture in nets pose lethal dangers to these animals.

Recognizing the urgency to protect these incredible creatures, numerous conservation efforts are underway in South Eastern Alaska. Government agencies, environmental organizations, and local communities are actively working together to establish marine protected areas, where sea mammals can find refuge and thrive undisturbed. These protected areas not only provide a safe haven for the animals but also help to preserve their natural habitats and the delicate balance of the marine ecosystem.

Public awareness campaigns and educational programs are also essential components of conservation efforts. By informing and engaging the public, these initiatives aim to foster a sense of responsibility and encourage individuals to adopt sustainable practices that reduce pollution and protect sea mammal habitats.

It is crucial for everyone to recognize the significance of these common sea mammals in South Eastern Alaska and the urgent need for conservation. By supporting and participating in these efforts, we can ensure the survival and well-being of these magnificent creatures for generations to come. Together, we can preserve the natural beauty of this region and maintain the delicate balance of its marine ecosystem.

Responsible Behavior around Sea Mammals

As visitors to the beautiful wilderness of South Eastern Alaska, it is crucial for us to understand and practice responsible behavior around the common sea mammals that call this region home. These magnificent creatures, which include whales, seals, sea lions, and otters, are not only a vital part of the marine ecosystem but also a major attraction for tourists and residents alike. By following a few simple guidelines, we can ensure their safety and well-being, while also enjoying the unique experience of observing them in their natural habitat.

First and foremost, it is important to maintain a safe distance from these animals. Approaching too closely can cause them stress and disrupt their natural behaviors, potentially endangering both them and us. As a general rule, maintain a distance of at least 100 yards from whales, and 50 yards from seals, sea lions, and otters. This not only protects the animals but also keeps us safe from any unexpected behaviors they may exhibit.

When observing sea mammals, it is crucial to do so quietly and respectfully. Avoid making loud noises, sudden movements, or using flash photography, as these actions can startle and disturb them. By maintaining a calm and quiet demeanor, we can minimize our impact on their natural environment and ensure a more peaceful coexistence.

Feeding sea mammals is strictly prohibited. While it may be tempting to share your snacks or leftovers with them, this can disrupt their natural feeding patterns and cause dependency on human food. It is important to remember that these animals are perfectly capable of finding their own food in the wild, and interfering with this process can have negative long-term consequences for their health and survival.

Lastly, it is crucial to dispose of our waste properly. Litter, particularly plastic, poses a significant threat to sea mammals and other marine life. Always pack out what you pack in, and make sure to properly dispose of any trash in designated bins or recycling facilities. By keeping our surroundings clean, we can help protect the habitats of these incredible creatures.

By following these responsible behavior guidelines, we can ensure a harmonious and sustainable relationship with the common sea mammals of South Eastern Alaska. Let us all do our part to protect these magnificent creatures and preserve the beauty of our natural environment for generations to come.

Best Practices for Marine Mammal Watching

Introduction:

South Eastern Alaska is a haven for marine mammals, boasting a diverse array of species that call its waters home. From majestic humpback whales to playful sea otters, encountering these incredible creatures in their natural habitat is a thrilling experience for locals and visitors alike. However, it is essential to approach marine mammal watching responsibly and respectfully to ensure the well-being of these magnificent animals and to preserve their habitats for future generations. This subchapter will outline the best practices for marine mammal watching in South Eastern Alaska, providing guidelines for everyone to enjoy these encounters while minimizing disturbance and promoting conservation efforts.

1. Observe from a safe distance:
When observing marine mammals, it is crucial to maintain a safe distance to avoid causing stress or altering their natural behavior. Experts recommend staying at least 100 yards away from most species and increasing the distance to 300 yards for larger animals like whales. Using binoculars or zoom lenses can provide a closer view without intruding on their space.

2. Be mindful of noise pollution:
Excessive noise can disrupt marine mammals' communication, causing distress and potentially affecting their ability to find food or mates. When observing them, turn off engines or reduce speed to minimize noise pollution. Keep voices low and avoid sudden loud noises or music.

3. Do not feed or approach:
Feeding marine mammals can lead to dependency on humans or alter their natural diet, impacting their health and behavior. It is crucial to refrain from feeding or attempting to touch them. Similarly, avoid approaching them too closely, as it can cause stress and disrupt their natural patterns.

4. Respect restricted areas and seasons:
Certain areas or seasons may be designated as protected or sensitive to marine mammals. Respect these regulations to minimize disturbance and

support conservation efforts. Familiarize yourself with local guidelines and adhere to them strictly.

5. Consider joining guided tours:
Joining guided tours led by experienced naturalists and marine biologists is an excellent way to enhance your marine mammal watching experience. These experts can provide valuable insights into the behavior, conservation, and ecology of the species you encounter and ensure you follow the best practices.

Conclusion:
Marine mammal watching in South Eastern Alaska is a unique opportunity to witness the wonders of these extraordinary creatures in their natural environment. By following the best practices outlined in this subchapter, we can minimize disturbance, protect their habitats, and contribute to their conservation. Remember, every individual's responsible actions can make a significant difference in preserving the rich biodiversity and ensuring the future well-being of the common sea mammals of South Eastern Alaska.

Reporting Sightings and Contributing to Citizen Science

One of the most exciting aspects of exploring the common sea mammals of South Eastern Alaska is the opportunity to contribute to citizen science. Citizen science is a collaborative effort between scientists and the general public to gather data and contribute to scientific research. By reporting your sightings and observations, you can become an integral part of ongoing efforts to understand and protect these magnificent creatures.

Observing sea mammals in their natural habitat can be a thrilling experience, but it also holds great value for scientific research. Your sightings can provide valuable information about population distribution, behavior, and even help identify new species. Every sighting, no matter how small, can contribute to our understanding of these incredible creatures.

So, how can you contribute to citizen science? The first step is to become a keen observer. Pay attention to the details when you encounter sea mammals - note their behavior, location, and any distinguishing features. Take photographs or videos if possible, as these can provide additional evidence for researchers.

Once you have gathered your observations, it's time to report them. There are several platforms and organizations dedicated to collecting data on sea mammal sightings. These platforms often have user-friendly interfaces that allow you to input your data and contribute to ongoing research projects. Your reports can help scientists track the movement patterns of these animals, monitor population changes, and even assess the impact of human activities in their habitats.

In addition to reporting sightings, you can also participate in more structured citizen science initiatives. Some organizations offer training programs or workshops where you can learn how to collect data in a standardized manner. This ensures that your observations are comparable to those of other citizen scientists and can be used in scientific studies.

By contributing to citizen science, you become an active participant in the conservation efforts of common sea mammals in South Eastern Alaska. Your observations and data can inform policies that aim to protect these animals and their habitats. Together, we can make a difference and ensure the survival of these magnificent creatures for generations to come.

So, the next time you encounter a sea mammal in the wild, remember to report your sighting and contribute to citizen science. Your actions can help shape the future of these incredible creatures and the delicate ecosystems they inhabit.

Chapter 7: Resources for Further Exploration

Recommended Books and Field Guides

In the vast expanse of the South Eastern Alaskan waters, a remarkable world of sea mammals thrives. To delve deeper into this captivating realm, we have compiled a list of recommended books and field guides that will enhance your understanding and appreciation of the common sea mammals found in this region. Whether you are a passionate nature enthusiast, an aspiring marine biologist, or simply someone who seeks to connect with the wonders of nature, these resources are tailored to cater to your interests and provide a comprehensive exploration of the marine life in South Eastern Alaska.

1. "Marine Mammals of Alaska" by Kate Wynne: This extensively illustrated guidebook is a must-have for anyone interested in the diverse marine mammal species inhabiting Alaskan waters. Packed with detailed descriptions and vibrant photographs, it offers valuable insights into the behavior, distribution, and conservation status of these fascinating creatures.

2. "Whales, Dolphins, and Porpoises of the Pacific Northwest" by Tamara Eder: Focusing on the cetaceans of the Pacific Northwest, including South Eastern Alaska, this book provides a comprehensive overview of the region's whale, dolphin, and porpoise species. It covers identification, behavior, and natural history, making it an ideal companion for any sea mammal enthusiast.

3. "Field Guide to Marine Mammals of the Pacific Coast" by Sarah Allen and Joe Mortenson: This handy field guide is perfect for those looking to identify and learn about the marine mammals encountered along the Pacific Coast, including South Eastern Alaska. With detailed illustrations and informative text, it offers a wealth of information on species such as sea otters, seals, and sea lions.

4. "Alaska's Watchable Whales" by Mark Kelley: Delve into the world of Alaska's magnificent whales with this visually stunning guidebook. Filled with breathtaking photographs and captivating narratives, it showcases the

beauty and grandeur of these gentle giants, making it an ideal companion for any nature lover.

5. "Guide to Marine Mammals of Alaska" by Karyn Rode: This comprehensive guide provides an in-depth look into the marine mammals of Alaska, including their biology, ecology, and conservation. It offers valuable information on species such as humpback whales, harbor seals, and Steller sea lions, making it an essential resource for those seeking a deeper understanding of these remarkable creatures.

By immersing yourself in these recommended books and field guides, you will unlock a wealth of knowledge about the common sea mammals of South Eastern Alaska. Whether you are planning a visit to this awe-inspiring region or simply wish to expand your knowledge, these resources will undoubtedly enrich your understanding and appreciation of the diverse marine life that calls this place home. So, grab a book, embark on a journey of discovery, and let the wonders of South Eastern Alaska's sea mammals captivate your imagination.

Websites and Online Databases

In this digital age, the internet has become an invaluable resource for accessing information on various topics, and the world of marine life is no exception. When it comes to exploring the common sea mammals of South Eastern Alaska, websites and online databases offer an abundance of knowledge and resources for everyone interested in these fascinating creatures.

One of the most reliable sources to learn about sea mammals is through dedicated websites that focus on marine life. These websites provide detailed information about different species of sea mammals found in South Eastern Alaska, their habitats, behaviors, and conservation efforts. They often feature stunning photographs and videos that bring these majestic creatures to life, allowing you to witness their beauty and grace from the comfort of your own home.

https://www.adfg.alaska.gov/index.cfm?adfg=viewing.marinemammals

Online databases are another essential tool for anyone seeking comprehensive information about sea mammals. These databases compile scientific research, studies, and observations made by marine biologists and researchers. They offer a wealth of information on the biology, ecology, and distribution of different species, helping to deepen our understanding of these animals and their role in the ecosystem.

These websites and databases are not just reserved for experts and scientists; they are accessible to everyone. Whether you are a student, a nature enthusiast, or someone planning a trip to South Eastern Alaska, these online resources can provide valuable insights and help you make the most of your experience.

For researchers and conservationists, these online platforms offer an opportunity to contribute to ongoing efforts. Many websites and databases encourage citizen science initiatives, where individuals can report sightings, share photographs, or participate in data collection programs. By actively engaging with these platforms, you can contribute to the knowledge base and aid in the conservation of these amazing sea mammals.

In conclusion, websites and online databases are invaluable resources for anyone interested in learning about the common sea mammals of South Eastern Alaska. Whether you want to expand your knowledge, plan a trip, or contribute to conservation efforts, these online platforms offer a gateway to a world of information and opportunities. So, dive into the digital realm and embark on a virtual journey to explore the wonders of South Eastern Alaska's sea mammals.

Research Organizations and Conservation Efforts

In the vast and diverse waters of South Eastern Alaska, a multitude of common sea mammals thrive. These incredible creatures, ranging from whales to seals, otters to dolphins, are not only a source of wonder and awe but also play a crucial role in maintaining the delicate balance of the marine ecosystem. To ensure their protection and preservation, numerous research organizations and conservation efforts have been established.

One such organization making significant strides in the field of marine mammal research is the Alaska Marine Mammal Laboratory (AMML). This renowned institution focuses on studying the behavior, population dynamics, and overall health of sea mammals in the region. Through their dedicated efforts, they provide valuable insights into the lives of these animals, aiding in the development of effective conservation strategies.

The AMML utilizes various research techniques, including satellite tagging, genetic analysis, and acoustic monitoring, to gather data on the movements, feeding habits, and social structures of common sea mammals. This information is then used to better understand their ecological roles, identify potential threats, and propose measures for their protection. Through collaborations with other research organizations and government agencies, the AMML ensures that their findings contribute to the conservation efforts in South Eastern Alaska.

Conservation efforts in the region extend beyond research organizations, with a range of initiatives aimed at safeguarding the common sea mammals. One such initiative is the establishment of marine protected areas (MPAs) that serve as sanctuaries for these animals. These designated areas restrict human activities, such as fishing and boating, reducing the risk of habitat destruction and disturbance to the mammals' natural behaviors.

Additionally, public awareness campaigns and educational programs play a vital role in fostering a sense of responsibility and stewardship towards the marine environment. By educating locals and visitors alike about the importance of conserving these amazing creatures, these initiatives strive to create a community that values and respects the natural world.

The efforts of research organizations and conservation initiatives are crucial in ensuring the long-term survival of common sea mammals in South Eastern Alaska. By studying their behavior, advocating for their protection, and engaging the public, these organizations play a pivotal role in preserving the rich biodiversity and natural beauty of these waters for future generations.

Whether you are a marine enthusiast, a nature lover, or simply curious about the magnificent sea mammals of South Eastern Alaska, understanding the work being done by research organizations and conservation efforts is essential. By supporting these initiatives and spreading awareness, we can all contribute to the conservation and stewardship of these incredible creatures and their fragile habitats.

Chapter 8: Frequently Asked Questions about South Eastern Alaska's Sea Mammals

What is the best time of year to spot sea mammals in South Eastern Alaska?

South Eastern Alaska is renowned for its rich marine life, particularly its diverse population of sea mammals. From majestic humpback whales to playful sea otters, this region offers a unique opportunity to witness these incredible creatures up close. However, if you're planning a trip to South Eastern Alaska to catch a glimpse of these common sea mammals, it's essential to know the best time of year to maximize your chances of spotting them.

The prime time for sea mammal sightings in South Eastern Alaska is during the summer months, from May to September. This period coincides with the migration of several species, including humpback whales, orcas, and harbor seals, to the region's abundant feeding grounds. These charismatic creatures follow the seasonal influx of fish, making this time of year ideal for observing their natural behaviors.

May and June are particularly favorable months for spotting humpback whales as they return to Alaska's waters after their long migration from Hawaii, Japan, Mexico, and Costa Rica. These gentle giants can often be seen breaching and slapping their tails on the water's surface, creating a spectacle that is both awe-inspiring and humbling.

July and August are the best months to witness the incredible diversity of sea mammals in South Eastern Alaska. During this time, orcas, also known as killer whales, are frequently seen hunting in pods. Their distinct black and white markings make them easily identifiable, and the sight of these powerful creatures in action is truly unforgettable.

If you're interested in observing sea otters, September is an excellent time to visit. These playful animals can often be seen floating on their backs, using rocks as tools to crack open their favorite food, shellfish. Witnessing their clever and endearing behavior is a delightful experience for any nature enthusiast.

It's important to note that while summer offers the best chance of spotting sea mammals, wildlife sightings are never guaranteed. Factors such as weather conditions, whale migration patterns, and the availability of food can all influence the timing and frequency of sightings. However, by planning your trip during the recommended months, you significantly increase your chances of encountering these magnificent creatures in their natural habitat.

In conclusion, if you're eager to witness the common sea mammals of South Eastern Alaska, plan your visit between May and September. Be prepared for a truly remarkable experience as you witness humpback whales, orcas, sea otters, and more in their natural environment. Remember to respect their space and follow the guidelines to ensure the conservation of these incredible creatures for future generations to enjoy.

Are sea mammals dangerous to humans?

When it comes to the fascinating world of sea mammals, one question that often arises is whether these magnificent creatures pose any danger to humans. In this subchapter, we will explore the interactions between sea mammals and humans, specifically focusing on the common sea mammals found in the enchanting waters of South Eastern Alaska.

It is important to note that while sea mammals are generally not aggressive towards humans, they are wild animals and should be treated with respect and caution. Most interactions between humans and sea mammals occur during wildlife viewing tours or when individuals encounter them in their natural habitat.

Among the common sea mammals found in South Eastern Alaska, the most iconic and beloved are the humpback whales, orca whales, sea lions, and harbor seals. These majestic creatures are known for their beauty and grace, and encounters with them are often awe-inspiring. However, it is crucial to maintain a safe distance and adhere to guidelines set forth by wildlife authorities to avoid any potential harm to both humans and animals.

While rare, there have been instances where sea mammals have displayed aggressive behavior towards humans. It is essential to understand that these occurrences are exceptional and typically happen in unusual circumstances, such as when a sea mammal feels threatened or cornered. Understanding the signs of stress or discomfort in these animals can help humans maintain a safe distance and minimize any potential dangers.

For example, humpback whales are known for their playful nature, often breaching and slapping their tails on the water's surface. While these behaviors may seem harmless, it is vital to keep a safe distance to avoid accidental collisions. Similarly, orca whales, although highly intelligent and social, are powerful predators and should be admired from a distance.

Sea lions and harbor seals, on the other hand, are known to be curious and may approach humans, especially when fishing or cleaning their catch. While interactions with these mammals can be exhilarating, it is crucial to remember that they are still wild animals and should not be provoked or fed.

In conclusion, sea mammals found in South Eastern Alaska are generally not dangerous to humans. However, it is essential to treat them with respect and caution, maintaining a safe distance to ensure the safety of both humans and animals. By understanding their behaviors and following guidelines set by wildlife authorities, individuals can enjoy the wonders of observing these incredible creatures in their natural habitat while minimizing any potential risks.

How can I contribute to sea mammal conservation efforts?

Sea mammals play a vital role in maintaining the balance and health of our marine ecosystems. As residents and visitors of South Eastern Alaska, we have the privilege of sharing our waters with a diverse range of sea mammals, including whales, seals, sea lions, and otters. The conservation of these magnificent creatures is of utmost importance to ensure their survival and the preservation of our natural heritage. Here are some ways in which you can actively contribute to sea mammal conservation efforts:

1. Educate yourself: Knowledge is the first step towards making a positive impact. Take the time to learn about the various sea mammal species that inhabit the waters of South Eastern Alaska. Familiarize yourself with their unique characteristics, behaviors, and the threats they face. This will enable you to appreciate their importance and contribute effectively to their conservation.

2. Support local initiatives: Numerous organizations and research institutions are dedicated to the conservation of sea mammals in this region. Consider supporting their efforts through donations, volunteering, or participating in citizen science programs. These initiatives rely on public support to carry out vital research, rescue operations, and public awareness campaigns.

3. Be a responsible boater: If you are out on the water, be mindful of your actions and their potential impact on sea mammals. Maintain a safe distance from these animals, as approach distances are legally mandated

to prevent disturbance and harassment. Follow guidelines for responsible whale
watching and avoid excessive noise and sudden changes in speed or direction.

4. Reduce plastic pollution: Marine mammals are often victims of plastic pollution, which can entangle them or be ingested, leading to severe health issues. Reduce your plastic consumption, recycle properly, and participate in beach clean-ups to prevent plastic waste from entering the oceans.

5. Report sightings and incidents: If you spot a stranded, injured, or entangled sea mammal, report it to the appropriate authorities immediately. Quick action can save lives and ensure that injured animals receive the necessary care.

6. Promote sustainable fishing practices: Support local fisheries that employ sustainable fishing methods, as unsustainable practices can impact the availability of prey for sea mammals. By choosing sustainably sourced seafood, you contribute to maintaining a healthy marine ecosystem for these animals.

By taking these small but significant steps, we can all contribute to the conservation of the common sea mammals of South Eastern Alaska. Remember, our actions today will determine the future of these incredible creatures and the health of our oceans. Let's work together to protect and preserve these magnificent animals for generations to come.

The Ongoing Importance of Research and Conservation

In the vast wilderness of South Eastern Alaska, a realm of untamed beauty and diverse marine life, it is crucial to recognize the ongoing importance of research and conservation efforts. This subchapter aims to shed light on the significance of these endeavors, not only for the common sea mammals of this region but for all living beings.

South Eastern Alaska is home to a rich array of sea mammals, including humpback whales, sea otters, harbor seals, and Dall's porpoises, to name just a few. These magnificent creatures play a vital role in the delicate balance of the marine ecosystem. However, their populations have faced numerous challenges over the years, such as habitat degradation, climate change, and human activities.

Research serves as the foundation for understanding the behavior, population dynamics, and ecological roles of these sea mammals. It provides valuable insights into their migratory patterns, breeding habits, and feeding preferences. By studying their biology and ecology, researchers can identify potential threats and develop effective conservation strategies.

Conservation efforts are crucial to safeguarding the future of these magnificent creatures. This involves not only protecting their habitats but also addressing the wider environmental issues that impact their well-being. Through research, we can identify the specific habitats and feeding grounds that are critical for the survival of these animals, and take steps to preserve and restore them.

The ongoing importance of research and conservation extends far beyond the sea mammals of South Eastern Alaska. By protecting these creatures, we are also safeguarding the integrity of the entire marine ecosystem. Sea mammals are often considered "indicator species" – their health serves as a barometer for the overall health of the environment. By monitoring and protecting their populations, we can ensure the well-being of all marine life, including fish, crustaceans, and even humans who rely on these resources.

Moreover, research and conservation efforts provide opportunities for education and awareness. By sharing our knowledge and understanding of these creatures, we can foster a sense of stewardship and inspire a new generation of conservationists. It is through these collective efforts that we can create a sustainable future for South Eastern Alaska's common sea mammals and the entire marine ecosystem.

In conclusion, the ongoing importance of research and conservation for the common sea mammals of South Eastern Alaska cannot be overstated. Through research, we can deepen our understanding of these creatures and the threats they face. Conservation efforts are vital to protect their habitats and ensure their survival, while also safeguarding the health of the entire marine ecosystem. By recognizing the significance of these endeavors, we can work together to create a future where these magnificent creatures thrive and inspire generations to come.

Encouraging Future Generations to Appreciate and Protect Sea Mammals

Introduction:

In the vast waters of South Eastern Alaska, a diverse range of magnificent sea mammals call this region home. From the playful sea otters to the majestic humpback whales, these creatures captivate our imagination and remind us of the incredible beauty and importance of our oceans. This subchapter aims to encourage everyone, from locals to tourists, to appreciate and protect the common sea mammals of South Eastern Alaska.

Understanding the Importance:

Sea mammals play a crucial role in the balance of marine ecosystems.

They are not only fascinating to observe, but they also contribute to the health of our oceans. For instance, sea otters play a vital role in maintaining kelp forests, which serve as nurseries and habitats for a multitude of marine species. Similarly, humpback whales help regulate the abundance of krill and other small fish, ensuring a sustainable food chain.

Educating the Next Generation:

Instilling a love and appreciation for sea mammals in future generations is essential to their conservation. By introducing children to these incredible creatures through educational programs, interactive exhibits, and engaging activities, we can nurture their curiosity and inspire them to become stewards of the sea. Encouraging field trips, wildlife photography contests, and art exhibitions focused on sea mammals can also foster a deeper connection with these animals.

Responsible Tourism:

Tourism plays a significant role in the economy of South Eastern Alaska, attracting visitors from all over the world. However, it's crucial to promote responsible tourism practices that minimize disturbances to sea mammals. Educating tourists about maintaining a safe distance, not feeding the animals, and reducing underwater noise pollution can help protect their natural behaviors and habitats.

Supporting Conservation Efforts:

To ensure the long-term survival of sea mammals, it is essential to support local organizations and initiatives dedicated to their conservation. By volunteering, donating, or participating in citizen science projects, individuals can actively contribute to research, rescue efforts, and habitat restoration programs. Additionally, advocating for stronger regulations and policies to protect sea mammals and their habitats can have a lasting impact.

Conclusion:

Appreciating and protecting the common sea mammals of South Eastern Alaska is a responsibility we all share. By understanding their importance, educating future generations, promoting responsible tourism, and supporting conservation efforts, we can ensure these magnificent creatures continue to thrive in the wild waters of Alaska. Let us come together, as stewards of the sea, to safeguard their future and preserve the incredible beauty of our oceans for generations to come.

Final Thoughts and Reflections

As we come to the end of this captivating journey through the fascinating world of South Eastern Alaska's common sea mammals, it is essential to reflect upon the incredible beauty and importance of these magnificent creatures. Through this field guide, we have aimed to provide everyone, from nature enthusiasts to researchers and tourists, with a deeper understanding and appreciation for the diverse marine life that inhabits this region.

The waters of South Eastern Alaska are teeming with an extraordinary variety of sea mammals, each playing a vital role in maintaining the delicate balance of this unique ecosystem. From the magnificent humpback whales, with their awe-inspiring acrobatics and haunting songs, to the adorable harbor seals that can be spotted basking on rocky shores, these mammals are a testament to the wonders of nature.

Through the chapters of this book, we have delved into the lives of these creatures, exploring their habitats, behaviors, and the challenges they face. It is our hope that by learning about their lives, we can inspire a sense of responsibility and conservation among our readers. The future of these common sea mammals relies heavily on our collective efforts to protect their habitat and ensure their survival for generations to come.

We must remember that the well-being of these sea mammals is intrinsically linked to the health of our oceans. The impacts of climate change, pollution, and overfishing pose significant threats to their survival. By taking small steps in our daily lives, such as reducing our carbon footprint and supporting sustainable fishing practices, we can contribute to the preservation of these remarkable creatures and their environment.

This field guide is just a starting point, a window into the world of South Eastern Alaska's common sea mammals. We encourage everyone to continue exploring, observing, and learning about these creatures firsthand. Witnessing a humpback whale breach or a playful sea otter floating on its back is an experience that will forever leave an imprint on your soul.

In conclusion, we invite you to cherish the knowledge gained from this guide and share it with others. Let us be ambassadors for the common sea mammals of South Eastern Alaska, advocating for their protection and understanding that their survival is intricately tied to our own. Together, we can ensure that future generations will continue to marvel at the wonders of these wild waters and the incredible creatures that call them home.

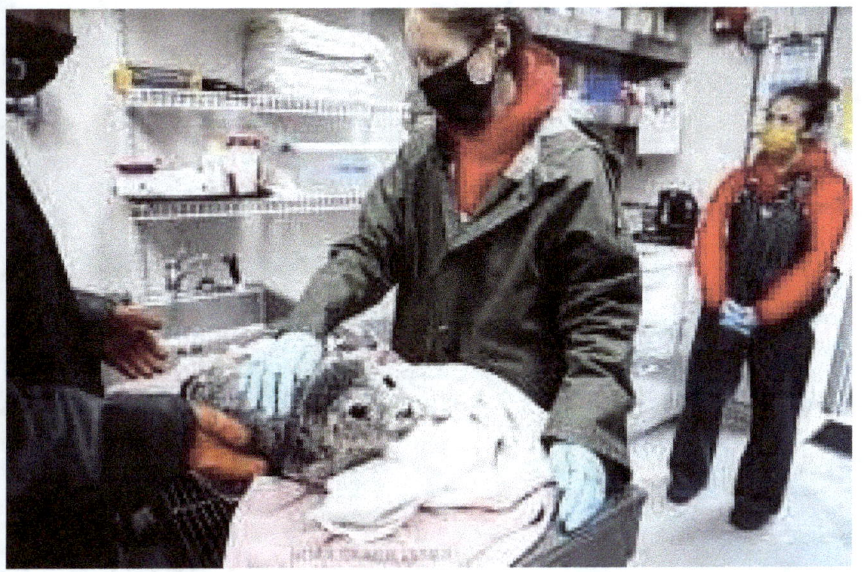

Bibliography

1. Wynne, Kate. Marine Mammals of Alaska. Fourth edition, Alaska Sea Grant College, 2013

2. https://www.adfg.alaska.gov/index.cfm?adfg=animals.listmammals

3. Allen, Sarah G. Mortenson, Joe. Webb, Sophie. Field Guide to Marine Mammals of the Pacific Coast. First edition, University of California Press, 2011

4. Kelly, Mark. Alaska's Watchable Whales: Humpback & Killer Whales. Second edition, Mark Kelley Publishing, 2016

About the Author

Frederick Grant studied Psychology-Neurobiology, Literature, and Linguistics at UCLA. He also studied Marine Biology, Ornithology, Botany, Zoology, and Geology at the University of Costa Rica. Additionally, he studied at the University of Wyoming obtaining an Outdoor Naturalist Certification, enabling him to work in Grand Teton NP, and in Yellowstone NP as a certified Naturalist. He has worked as a Naturalist, Lecturer, and Wildlife Expert in Alaska, Wyoming, Costa Rica, the Galapagos Islands, and the Sub Antarctic regions of South America.

South Eastern Alaska is a region renowned for its rich biodiversity and stunning natural landscapes. Nestled along the Pacific coast, this area is home to a plethora of common sea mammals, making it a haven for marine wildlife enthusiasts and nature lovers alike. In this book, we will delve into the diverse array of sea mammals found in this remarkable region, highlighting their unique characteristics and the importance of their conservation.

One of the most iconic sea mammals in South Eastern Alaska is the humpback whale. Known for their majestic breaches and haunting songs, these gentle giants migrate to the region during the summer months to feed on the nutrient-rich waters. Their distinctive flippers and long, white flukes make them easily recognizable, and witnessing their acrobatic displays is a true spectacle of nature.

Another common sea mammal found in these waters is the Steller sea lion. These charismatic creatures, with their thick fur and large, dark bodies, are a favorite among visitors to the region. Steller sea lions are known for their playful behavior and can often be spotted basking on rocky shores or gracefully swimming through the waves. However, due to habitat loss and overfishing, they are now considered a threatened species, emphasizing the need for conservation efforts.

South Eastern Alaska is also home to several species of seals, including the harbor seal and the spotted seal. Harbor seals, with their wide-eyed expressions and sleek bodies, can often be seen lounging on ice floes or rocky outcrops. These seals play an essential role in maintaining the delicate balance of the marine ecosystem and are a vital part of the region's biodiversity.

In addition to these well-known sea mammals, South Eastern Alaska is teeming with other fascinating creatures such as orcas, Dall's porpoises, and sea otters. Each species contributes to the intricate web of life in this region, and their presence is a testament to the importance of preserving the natural environment.

As responsible stewards of this planet, it is our duty to protect and conserve the rich biodiversity found in South Eastern Alaska. Understanding the unique characteristics and behaviors of these common sea mammals is the first step towards fostering a deep appreciation for their existence. By raising awareness and supporting conservation initiatives, we can ensure that generations to come will have the opportunity to marvel at the splendor of these remarkable creatures and the incredible natural wonders of South Eastern Alaska.